Building Foundations Publishing Company
One Battery Park Plaza
Floor 18
New York, New York 10004

Special discounts are available on quantity purchases by corporations, associations, and others. For details, contact the publisher at the address above. For information on orders by U.S. trade bookstores and wholesalers, please contact Building Foundations Publishing Company; Tel: (212) 825-0365; Email: info@buildingfoundationspublishing.com; or visit www.buildingfoundationspublishing.com.

Library of Congress Cataloging-in-Publication Data
Bailey, Adam Leitman.
Home / Adam Leitman Bailey.
p. cm.
ISBN 978-0-9995704-0-1
1. Children's literature — Family. 2. Children's literature — Homes.
3. Fiction — Children and families. 4. Fiction — Homes. I. Title.
II. Bailey, Adam Leitman.

Library of Congress Control Number: 2018934184

First Edition

10 9 8 7 6 5 4 3 2 1

Printed in China

Building Foundations Publishing Company aims to inspire and educate children through its books.

DEDICATION

To all of the children who know that living with your family and the love you receive from them is much more important than the size of your home;

To the most magnificent mother, who gives so much love that any child will forget about what he or she does not have, Jennifer Leitman Bailey;

And to our little boys Benjamin and Nathaniel who have inspired this book and myself in so many ways that if I wrote about them in a book, no one would believe the story.

HOME

Written by Adam Leitman Bailey

There once was a boy. He lived with his family in a small, small apartment in a big, big city. A city filled with people and cars, buildings and parks.

The boy looked out his tall window and

could see all kinds of different homes.

He wanted to see if he could find a nicer place to

live. He told his family his idea and off he went.

First, the boy visited a large house with a huge driveway.

It even had its own basketball court and the rooms inside

were very large. Outside, there was a lot of green grass.

And in the backyard sat a big blue swimming pool.

Next, the boy visited a big farm filled with many animals.

Among other animals, the boy saw sheep, goats, pigs, ducks, and cows.

On the other side of the farm, the boy met a farmer.

The farmer showed him where all the plants and

vegetables grew and even gave him some corn to eat.

The farmer showed him how to milk a cow. Then he

gave the boy some milk to drink. It was warm, sweet,

and delicious.

After the farm, the boy visited a mobile home. Many

mobile homes shared a large piece of land.

He saw lots of boys and girls playing games together,

and he joined in.

Next, the boy found a bird's nest in the branches of a small tree. The nest was made out of plant stems and straw, long pieces of grass, and reeds. The birds had made these into a circle. Next to the nest, the boy saw two large birds, and inside were a baby bird and two eggs.

Although the nest seemed to be very cozy,

the boy wondered if it was just too small to fit his

books and toys.

Finally, the boy visited a house on a lake. On this very

large lake, the people used a boat to travel.

The boys and girls there could play all day in the water,

swimming, fishing, canoeing, and enjoying the outdoors.

Although the boy thought all of these homes were fun,

he missed his small, small apartment in the big, big

city. So the boy ran into his apartment and hugged his

parents, knowing that in the entire world, his home

was the best place for him because that was where his

family lived.

He realized that it was not about the size of the home.

And it was not about how much fun the people who lived

there had. His family was what made his apartment a

home and a wonderful place to live, and the boy knew

that his family loved him very, very much.

About the Author

Adam Leitman Bailey is a best-selling and award-winning author, and a doting father.